The Trouble with Our State

The Trouble with Our State

Daniel Berrigan

Edited with a Foreword by John Dear

Introduction by Bill Wylie-Kellermann

RESOURCE *Publications* · Eugene, Oregon

THE TROUBLE WITH OUR STATE

Resource Publications
An Imprint of Wipf and Stock Publishers
199 W. 8th Ave., Suite 3
Eugene, OR 97401

www.wipfandstock.com

PAPERBACK ISBN: 978-1-6667-2950-4
HARDCOVER ISBN: 978-1-6667-2094-5
EBOOK ISBN: 978-1-6667-2095-2

AUGUST 27, 2021

For more information, visit www.danielberrigan.org.

For Carla Berrigan and Marc Pittarelli,

Friends and Peacemakers

"For me, Father Daniel Berrigan is Jesus as a poet."

—KURT VONNEGUT

What we are living through in the United States is so irrational and so incomprehensible to the majority of our people that one constantly has the sense of being in the middle of a nightmare which has no termination and no inner coherence.

~

One cannot level one's moral lance at every evil in the universe. There's are just too many of them. But you can do something and the difference between doing something and doing nothing is everything.

~

What are we to do with our lives? A question which seems to me is a peerless source of freedom to the one who dares pose it with seriousness. Anything short of confronting this question ends up sooner or later in a suffocating dead end. We have taken up one after another almost every question except the one which would liberate us: the question of our humanity. How is a human being to live today? How is he or she to live? Is it possible for a person to do something other than kill his brother or sister—the practically universal demand laid upon us by the state, approved by the silent church? Is there another way to live here and now, which will also allow future generations to live their lives in a different way from the one way sanctioned today?

~

One is called to live nonviolently, even if the change one works for seems impossible. It may or may not be possible to turn the U.S. around through nonviolent revolution. But one thing favors such an attempt: the total inability of violence to change anything for the better.

~

Nonviolence first and foremost, with its fiery trail of implication: compassion for the adversary, care of one another, community discipline, prayer and sacrament and biblical literary. Long term carefulness and short, care of little matters and large, the short run and the long It was easy to set down a formula, and devilishly hard to live by it, even in minor matters.

~

The only message I have to the world is: We are not allowed to kill innocent people. We are not allowed to be complicit in murder. We are not allowed to be silent while preparations for mass murder proceed in our name, with our money, secretly.

—DANIEL BERRIGAN

Contents

~

THE TROUBLE WITH OUR STATE

Foreword

John Dear

FATHER DANIEL BERRIGAN BECAME world famous in the late 1960s for his bold, public stand against the Vietnam War, along with his brother Philip, when the Catonsville Nine walked into a draft board office near Baltimore, Maryland, took some 300 draft files, brought them outside to the parking lot, poured homemade napalm on them, and then, in front of TV cameras, set them ablaze. No priests have ever done such a public act of resistance in the history of the United States.

"Our apologies, good friends, for the burning of paper instead of children," Dan's famous statement began. "We could not, so help us God, do otherwise." It would become, I submit, one of the greatest in resistance literature.

The photo of the nine resisters, including the two priest brothers, taken on May 17, 1968, appeared on the front page of newspapers around the country. Later, they were tried, convicted and found guilty. Dan, however, refused to submit to prison, and traveled underground for over four months, appearing regularly in public on the evening news and elsewhere, until he was arrested on August 11, 1970 on Block Island, Rhode Island, when he began two years in Danbury prison.

On September 9, 1980, Dan and Phil Berrigan were at it again. With six friends, they strolled into the G.E. nuclear weapons plant near Philadelphia along with other workers reporting to start their day building nuclear weapons. They proceeded calmly down the hallways through the plant and came across a room with unarmed nuclear weapons in it. They then proceeded to take out hammers and hammer on one to fulfill, they said, the prophet Isaiah's oracle, "They shall beat their swords into plowshares and their spears into pruning hooks and study war no more." With that, they were arrested and faced many more years in prison, and launched over one hundred similar plowshares disarmament actions that continue to this day.

Dan's peacemaking life has been well documented. After his death on April 30, 2016, just before his 95th birthday, his obituary was announced in every newspaper in the country, including the front page of *The New York Times, The Washington Post*, and the *L.A. Times*. He wrote over fifty books, was arrested over 200 times, influenced a generation of peacemakers, and pushed the churches to step up their witness for peace and nonviolence.

But before all of that, Daniel Berrigan was first of all a world class, award-winning poet. His first book of poetry, *Time Without Number,* in the late 1950s, published at the recommendation of the poet Marianne Moore, won the Lamott Poetry Award and was nominated for a National Book Award. With that, Daniel Berrigan was launched, known and loved by major and minor poets and ordinary church folk, too. His poetry spanned his peacemaking life, until the death of his brother Philip in 2002. After that, he told me, he could never write another poem again.

I first met Dan in the early 1980s as a young Jesuit, and saw in him an heir to St. Peter and St. Paul, as well as Gerard Manley Hopkins and Gandhi. From then on, I sat at his feet to learn from this holy apostle of peace. In the late 1990s, I gathered together all his poems in one big volume called "And the Risen Bread." Later, I published "Daniel Berrigan: Essential Writings," a beautiful collection of prose and poetry that will hold up for centuries, calling Christians to new heights of Christ's nonviolence. Long before he died, he arranged that I should be his literary executor and chair his literary estate.

This year, on May 9th, marks his 100th birthday, so I offer this collection of some of his best in-your-face, civilly disobedient, politically resistant poems, many from prison or about his brother Philip in prison, some of which have never before been published.

That's why I picked this title, after one of my favorite poems, "The Trouble with Our State." There, my friend calls us beyond our ignorant, apathetic, deadly "civil obedience" to our empire toward a more Christian, as well as Gandhian/Kingian nonviolent civil disobedience to all things legally evil, including racism, poverty, corporate greed, executions, war, nuclear weapons and environmental destruction, so that we can get on with the Gospel work of the Paschal Mystery and create a new culture of nonviolence.

In this collection, I've brought together some of his most well-known political poems, poems from prison, poems from resistance, and a few never before published. I hope they will inspire us to take up where Daniel Berrigan left off—following the nonviolent Jesus by resisting the culture of war, racism, nuclear weapons and environmental destruction and pursuing a new culture of justice, disarmament and environmental sustainability.

May we heed his call and carry on the Gospel journey of civil disobedience, creative nonviolence and divine obedience, to "seed hope," "flower peace," and trace "a liberated zone of paradise."

—Fr. John Dear
May 9, 2021
100th birthday of Daniel Berrigan

Introduction

Bill Wylie-Kellermann

"Remember, now, that the state has only one power it can use against you, against human beings: death. The state can persecute you, prosecute you, imprison you, exile you, execute you, all of these mean the same thing. The state can consign you to death. The grace of Jesus Christ in this life is that death fails. There is nothing the state can do to you or to me which we need fear."

SO SAID WILLIAM STRINGFELLOW at the evening Festival of Hope during the 1968 trial of the Catonsville Nine. His friend, Daniel Berrigan, then himself on trial, later summarized it with a line from Dylan Thomas (though echoing St. Paul): "Death shall have no dominion." Either would be a suitable introit to these selected poems. Together they utter the freedom of resurrection.

From Daniel Berrigan, I picked up that our task was not so much to put more politics into our poetry, but more poetry into our politics. Now comes a selection which compresses the two. Previous collections, including an earlier one edited by John Dear himself, have either been more sweeping in scope or more bound to a moment. This one covers a certain breadth of Dan's writing life, but the selections are conditioned with an eye to state and empire, seeing its weaponry, the endless wars of necessity, and resistance to them.

The title poem, from a clutch of nine he wrote while teaching just three weeks at Georgetown University (others of which are included as well), is a stark and straightforward call to civil disobedience. Or, at very least, to shake off the institutional assaults and seductions of a deadly lockstep: civil obedience. It too is a fitting way in.

As keeper of Dan's literary keys, few would know his corpus of poems better than John Dear. Beginning with a couple of later poems, his selection by and large follows a chronological organization. So, beginning with the momentous experiences of 1968, they silhouette his life, a biography of faith, and suggest a rhythm: community, action, trial, incarceration, community, action . . . all with pen in hand.

This selection is disciplined by the times. As Dan put it, in one of those trials (for Plowshares), testifying on the stand:

> It's terrible for me to live in a time where I have nothing to say to human beings except, "Stop killing." There are other beautiful things that I would love to be saying to people. There are other projects I could be very helpful at. And I can't do them. I cannot. Because everything is endangered. Everything is up for grabs. Ours is a kind of primitive situation, even though we would call ourselves sophisticated. Our plight is very primitive from a Christian point of view. We are back where we started. Thou shalt not kill; we are not allowed to kill. Everything today comes down to that — everything."

Now, hold that together with this:

> I believe we were created for ecstasy. And redeemed for it, at considerable cost. Certain vagrant unrepeatable moments of life tell us this, if we will but attend. Such moments, moreover, are clues to the native structure and texture of things. Not merely are such glorious fits and starts meant to 'keep us going,' a fairly unattractive idea; but ecstasy fuels and infuses us from the start, our proper distillation and energy of soul. One could dream the world, the poet says, and one could even dream the eye; but who can imagine the act of seeing? We will never have enough of this, we will never have done with it.

Hence this book. As poet (and prophet, if you will) I think of Daniel as a seer, in the mode of John, imprisoned on Patmos, and under a charge to "Write what you see . . . " (Rev. 1:11). One of his gifts is to see much. Watch for it herein.

On the one hand, there is a certain concise visual element to his poetry (so love doesn't merely reach, it strides) though he is modest about this gift.

All kinds of poets, believe me, could better praise your
sovereign beauty, your altogether subtle translation
of blank nature—
So that winds, nights, sunlight
(extraordinarily colorless phenomena) are drawn into
what can only be called a "new game."
Well, I will not revel
in humiliation. Yeats, Wordsworth would have looked once
breathed deeply, gone home, sharpened quills,
With a flourish plucked you from time.
But.
You are jailyard blooms . . .

I think likewise of his repeated collaborations, political and poetic,
with visual artists. Sometimes the art followed the verse. For "What Mar-
vels the Lord Works for Them," a Psalm poem included from *Uncommon
Prayer,* we are missing here Robert McGovern's companion woodcut of a
prisoner walking free in light fractiled by bars. Corita Kent was notorious
for taking Dan's one-liners and turning them into poster silk-screens with
great splashes of color.

In other cases, the art preceded, and Dan's poetry was a meditation
on the proffered image. He once did a book of poems *Stations: The Way
of the Cross*, based on clay relief panels by Margaret Parker, of the thirteen
"stations" framed as homeless folk in the subway. In the volume at hand,
"The Cross as Military Decoration," was written in Danbury Prison. A set
of paintings and paper laid images, by Gregory and Deborah Harris, de-
picting the symbolics of the cross (hidden and explicit, lifted and twisted)
were gotten into him for writing meditation. Forbidden to publish while
imprisoned, he nevertheless sent out letters in poetry and prose, which
when stitched together made the text of *Jesus Christ.* As to other such col-
laborators, I readily think of George Knowlton and fellow Jesuit iconogra-
pher, Bill McNichols.

But chief among them would be Tom Lewis, an artist, teacher and
Catholic Worker who was a participant in both the Baltimore Four and
the Catonsville Nine draft board actions. Together they shared community
and an apocalyptic style. A little-known, long, and by my lights, important
poem is included here: "A Letter from Prison to Vietnamese Prisoners." It
was published by the Hoa Binh Press, an arm of the N.Y. Thomas Merton
Center in 1972. With photographic collage, pen and ink illustrations by
Lewis, the eight poster-size pages fit together as a single work. It hangs so

on my study wall. That poem formed me personally when I committed it entire to memory. Let me consider it here.

Looking back, from Danbury, it names the reason for Catonsville and even a description of the action.

> . . . it must be insisted
> with equally rigorous logic;
> the murder of a child is sufficient reason
> to burn like trash or offal
> those hunting licenses
> that go by the civilized
> euphemism, "draft files," to endure
> imprisonment, loss of repute
> the stigma of Cain
> branded by the perfumed hands
> of judges, politicians and church men
> on the forehead of Abel.

And in the process, it brings prisoners halfway round the planet, close as face to face.

> Dear friends, your faces are a constriction of grief in the throat
> your words weigh us like chains, your tears and blood
> fall on our faces. Prison, Vietnam; Prison, U.S.
> Prison is our fate, mothers bear in prison,
> our tongues taste its gall, bars spring up
> from dragons' teeth, a paling, impaling us.

That last line echoes a poem of Thich Nhat Hanh's, "Fires spring up from dragon's teeth at the ten points of the universe." Nhat Hanh was surely the intermediary, multiplying and scattering this letter through Paris to the tiger cage prisoners and their communities. Hope is in the letter, but it is one squeezed out and in through the bars. It bears beneath the dark and heavy weight of the war and its spiritual consequence. It strikes as grief: the table community of Buddha and Christ spirals away lost in amnesia and death, a center which seems not to hold. A beatitude vision of the kin-dom recedes, hemmed in with the violence of powers. And their minions face the comeuppance of judgement.

> And we shall break our chains like chains of sand
>   the conniving dissolute
> puppets, their power
>   slumps like a rotten sawdust

their marauding hearts
     burst in a suppuration!

Of himself Dan once put it:

> I also write poetry, because it is a way of submitting my anger to
> a strict discipline. I do not want to live in the world and not be
> angry; neither do I want to die just yet. Nor do I want my anger to
> burn useless like a waste flame from an oil stack. Wanting to live,
> nursing my flame, I write. It is a way of surviving.

How much anger, hope wrestling despair, is disciplined in this poem
or others? "Thus far corruption on high/ of the call and the course of the
blood."

John Dear follows this with another, equally long and more well-
known poem from Danbury, "The Risen Tin Can." I first thought this a
shrewd placement. It has a lightness, almost whimsy, offering resurrection
and relief poised in the aftermath. Take a breath, it says.

But more. I only notice now that the two were written perhaps in
roughly the same period, indeed both reference Christmastide in prison.
This poem, so explicitly about resurrection, does sit aright here. It names
the task of the poet crushed, entombed: arise!

> But I digress.
>   The unforgiveable sin against the unholy Spirit
> Is the metamorphosis of tin
>   Into humanity
> Of which one instance: the writing of a poem.

Poetry as a resurrection deed. Yet, even more. These two poems share
a common line. "No to their No. Yes to all else." It was first in the Risen Tin
Can and subsequently added as a closing word of commitment, to the final
version of the Prison Letter, confirming that these two Danbury poems,
apocalyptic and whimsical, ought indeed be read together as companions.
The Yes is certainly the great Yes of Christ to humanity and all creation (as
per St. Paul; 2 Cor. 1:18-19).

However, "No to their No" bears further observation. It most simply
puts nonviolent resistance. Dan has a fondness or proclivity for double
negatives. "Non-violence," of course, is a double negative compressed into
a single word. Just so, he can name the fidelity of friendship, "non-betrayal."
Testifying in court to the compulsion of the Holy Spirit: "We could not not
do this!" There was an earlier version of that in the Catonsville statement:

"We could not, so help us God, do otherwise." Of crocodile judges and their statutes. "not letting me/not/let blood" (see p. 3). Or defining faith by a line from Graham Green, "This saves me,/ I don't believe my disbelief" (see p. 114). Thus. A Yes in a double No.

For making so much good trouble, for troubling the state of war, it's no surprise that so many of this collection originate in jail. Dan once told Jim Forest, friend and biographer, that "I should have gone to prison sooner. It's a pressure cooker of poetry."

In looking over the selections, I'm thinking of poetry and nonviolence. There is certainly the matter of bringing more poetics to action, for which Berrigan enjoys virtually a charism. This is not just in the recounting, plucking an action from the street and telling it in verse (there are any number of such here), but for casting actions in symbol, metaphor, liturgy, even sacrament. Enact the poem; embody it.

Poetry also has a freedom about it, akin to what Gandhi called non-attachment to results. Like prayer, or sacrament for that matter, one offers a poem into the world, setting it loose and letting it go. It is. A germinating seed. In that sense, this book is a seed packet of nonviolent resistance. The sower has cast it. Upon Earth. Upon us all.

At a birthday party for Dan, Kurt Vonnegut once quipped, "for me Dan Berrigan is Jesus as poet." I share the assessment. It serves as endorsement of this book. I am, however, quick to add that when it comes to endlessly unpacking the metaphor of his parables, we might notice Jesus had an inspired knack for it himself.

This selection honors the 100th birthday of our beloved poet. For that, a thanks to John Dear.

It is a joyous and demanding celebration. To it may all of us rise.

—Bill Wylie-Kellermann
May, 2021

The Trouble with Our State

The trouble with our state
was not civil disobedience
which in any case was hesitant and rare

Civil disobedience was rare as kidney stone
No, rarer; it was disappearing like immigrants' disease

You've heard of a war on cancer?
There is no war like the plague of media
There is no war like routine
There is no war like 3 square meals
There is no war like a prevailing wind

It blows softly; whispers
Don't rock the boat!
The sails obey, the ship of state rolls on.

The trouble with our state
—we learned it only afterward
when the dead resembled the living who resembled the dead
and civil virtue shone like paint on tin
and tin citizens and tin soldiers marched to the common whip

—our trouble
the trouble with our state
with our state of soul
our state of siege—
was
civil
obedience

Prophecy

The way I see the world is strictly illegal
To wit, through my eyes

is illegal, yes;
to wit, I live
like a pickpocket, like the sun
like the hand that writes this, by my wits

This is not permitted
that I look on the world
and worse, insist that I see

what I see
—a conundrum, a fury, a burning bush

and with five fingers, where my eyes fail
trace—

with a blackened brush
on butcher sheets, black on white
(black for blood, white for death
where the light fails)

—that face which is not my own
(and my own)
that death which is not my own
(and my own)

This is strictly illegal
and will land me in trouble

as somewhere now, in a precinct
in a dock, the statutes
thrash in fury, hear them

hear ye!
the majestic jaws

of crocodiles in black shrouds
the laws
forbidding me
the world, the truth
under blood oath

forbidding, row upon row
of razors, of statutes
of molars, of grinders—

those bloodshot eyes
legal, sleepless, maneating

—not letting me

not

let blood

Peacemaking Is Hard

hard almost as war.

the difference being one
we can stake life upon
and limb and thought and love.

I stake this poem out
dead man to a dead stick
to tempt an Easter chance—
if faith may be
truth, our evil chance
penultimate at last,

not last. We are not lost.

When these lines gathered
of no resource at all
serenity and strength,
it dawned on me

a man stood on his nails,

an ash like dew, a sweat
smelling of death and life.
Our evil Friday fled,
the blind face gently turned
another way. Toward Life.

A man walks in his shroud.

Children in the Shelter

Imagine: three of them.

As though survival
were a rat's word,
and a rat's death
waited there at the end

and I must have
in the century's boneyard
heft of flesh and bone in my hands

I picked up the littlest
a boy, his face
breaded with rice (his sister calmly feeding him
as we climbed down)

in my arms fathered
in a moment's grace, the messiah
of all my tears. I bore, reborn

a Hiroshima child from hell.

My Name

If I were Pablo Neruda
or William Blake
I could bear, and be eloquent

an American name in the world
where men perish
in our two murderous hands

Alas Berrigan
you must open those hands
and see, stigmatized in their palms,
the broken faces
you yearn toward

You cannot offer
being powerless as a woman
under the rain of fire—
life, the cover of your body.

Only the innocent die.
Take up, take up
the bloody map of the century.
the long trek homeward begins
into the land of unknowing.

The Death of the Children

(Once, after dinner at the Kennedys, Dan was asked to debate Secretary of Defense Robert McNamara. "Since Mr. McNamara didn't end the war this morning, he should end it this evening," Dan said. "Vietnam is Mississippi. When there's trouble, you send in the troops . . . ." Mr. McNamara said, to the shock of Dan.)

In my ignorant salad days
(the middle 60's), the wife of the Sec. of Defense
earnest, elegant as a pompeian matron
supped next to me.   Much admired
for D.C. school reform   a committeewoman
of fervor
    Her husband less admired
a cost product expert   hair slick as a beaver's
cold eyes instantly contracting to
the fleering public glare
    expanding
in the subterranean
warrens where he like a children's
animal tail
    disappeared around
this or that pentagonal corner

leaving the subaltern mice and moles
a-quiver to their nose hairs with
puritan angst   O how
(wail) quite measure up?

Fridays the pentagon prayer room was crowded

In the postprandial mellow summer dark (quote)
"Mississippi is Vietnam. When a people
reneges on joining the civilized world,
you send in the troops."

Providence has assigned
sons and daughter to the estimable pair.
My poem concerns
The death of children.

Wings

We flew in for trial.
A butterfly   came to rest on our big
Boeing wing
pushed there, a hand in ballet motion, a heartbeat.
I wished the little tacker luck. He was
technologically innocent, flying
by grace of the US Air Control Command
because his wing-spread
(I checked this)
lay somewhere below the danger area
of the breadth
of minor aircraft.

Eucharist

7 a.m. trial day,
courtesy of Warden Foster,
the San Jose vineyards
and a common baking shop,
we took
in a workman's cracked cup
at a slum table

prisoners' pot luck

The Verdict

Everything before was a great lie.
Illusion, distemper, the judge's eye
black and Jew for rigorists,
spontaneous vengeance. The children die
singing in the furnace. They say in hell
heaven is a great lie.

　　　　Years, years ago
my mother moves in youth. In her
I move too, to birth, to youth, to this.
The judge's *tic toc* is time's steel hand
summoning; *come priest from the priest hole, Risk!*
Everything else
Is a great lie. Four walls, home, love, youth,
truth untried, all, all is a great lie.
The truth the judge shuts in his two eyes.

Come Jesuit, the university cannot
no nor the universe, nor vatic Jesus
Imagine. Imagine! Everything before
was a great lie.

　　　　Philip, your freedom
stature, simplicity, the ghetto where the children
malinger, die—

　　　　Judge Thomsen
strike, strike with a hot hammer
the hour, the truth. The truth has birth
all former truth must die. Everything
before; all faith and hope, and love itself
was a great lie.

The Sermon on the Mount, and
The War That Will Not End Forever

Jesus came down from Crough Patrick
crazy with cold, starry with vision.
The sun undid what the moon did; unlocked him.

Light headed ecstasy; *love*
he commended, as tongue and teeth
fixed on it; *love* for meat after fast;

then *poverty, &*
mild and clean hearts stood commended.

Next spring, mounted Crough Patrick
and perished.
The word came down
comes down and down, comes what he said
men say, gainsay, say nay.

Not easy for those who man
the mountain, forever ringed and fired.
And the children, the children
                              die
die like our last chance
                    day
                        after Christian day

Certain Occult Utterances from the Underground and Its Guardian Sphinx

If you seek pleasure in everything
you must seek pleasure in nothing

If you wish to possess everything
you must desire to possess nothing

If you wish to become all
you must desire to be nothing

If you wish to know all
you must desire to know nothing

If you wish to arrive where you know not
you must go by a way you know not

If you wish to possess what you do not
you must dispossess

If you wish to become new
you must become as dead

A Penny Primer in the Art of Forgetfulness

What is the price of the future?
Forgetting the future

What is the price of revolution?
Forgetting the revolution

What things are to be forgotten?
The good things

Only?
Also the evil things

All things?
All things

What good things for instance?
Father   mother   family   friends

Also books   tastes   a settle abode
the view at the window
ecstasy   flowers
the truth and tide of season

What bad things?
offenses   hurts   foolishness   also
instinctive lunges   settled enmities
termites   rank offenses   shark mouths
the stuttering etc of nightmare

What is the value of this?
Connection

Where will it lead?
Forget where it will lead

You ask me to become a boor
an aardvark an amputee?
No. A Human.

How a human?
A human is one enabled
to forget
both method and way
                    consumed
in the act & grace of the human
the entire gift

What gift act grace?
We must borrow
one outlawed debased word—
Love

And then?
then then then

run off   empty your mind
like a dawn slops
or I shall I swear
by the Zen fathers
thwack your dense shoulders
with this bamboo

I Will Sign My Name

Now what the hell sort of dog's life is left to limp?
I may not mean what I see.
The FBI has devised for this emergency a poetry censor
whose eyes flame like an alcoholic's,
       smoke like Beelzebub's dry ice or dry armpit
when the bubonic smell of a poetic name-place
       falls under its snub snout.
I may not name river.
No, nor mountain, street, alley nor valley.
at least I will sign my name.
Now hold your nose, eyes, ears,
       in a one-mile perimeter of infernal headquarters.
All hell will shortly like dull scissors and sirens
       gouge, saw, at the inner ear.
Ready? Set? Then.
       Daniel Berrigan.

Seminar

One speaker
an impeccable Californian
impelled to explain

The Chinese belong in China
The Russians in Russia.
We however—
Messiah oversoul
A pink   muscled   clear-eyed
Texan dream, fumigating
Hanoi privies
From above—
Napalm   jigger bombs   gas
God's saniflush, in sum—

The gentleman was
four square as State
or the Pentateuch;
sans beard, rope, sandals, foul talk, pot—
a fire extinguisher on Pentecost,
exuding good will
like a mortician's convention
in a plague year.

Indeed yes.
There is nothing sick
(the corpse said)
about Death:
Come in.

Tulips in the Prison Yard

All kinds of poets, believe me, could better praise your
sovereign beauty, your altogether subtle translation
of blank nature—
　　　　So that winds, nights, sunlight
(extraordinarily colorless phenomena) are drawn into
what can only be called a "new game."
Well I will not revel
in humiliation. Yeats, Wordsworth would have looked once
breathed deeply, gone home, sharpened quills,
With a flourish plucked you from time.
　　　　But.
You are jailyard blooms, you wear bravery with a difference.
You are born here, will die here. Making you,
by excess of suffering
and transfiguration of suffering, ours.
I see prisoners pass
in dead spur of spring, before you show face.
Are you their glancing tears
the faces of wives and children,
the yin yang of hearts
to-fro like hanged necks,
in perpetual cruelty, absurdity?
　　　　The prisoners
pass and pass, shades of men, pre-men, khaki ghosts,
　　　　shame, futility.
Between smiles, between reason for smiles, between
life as fool's pace and life as celebrant's flame,
aeons.

Yet—thank you. Against the whips
of ignorant furies, the slavish pieties of judas priests
you stand, a first flicker in the brain's soil,
a precursor of judgment—

Dawn might be,
humanity may be
Or spelling it out in the hand's palm
of a blind mute:
God is fire,
is love.

Almost Everyone Is Dying Here.
Only a Few Actually Make It.

At 12:30 sharp
as though to underscore
some unassuageable grief
a man's head fell to one side
in the prison hospital.
No record of heart disease
a morning's weakness only. His neck went limp
in the pale March sunlight
like a wax man's
his hands opened, a beggar's hesitant reach
Before a rich man's shadow.
Near, there and
gone.

We Were Permitted to Meet Together in Prison to Prepare for Trial

Yesterday, the usual stiff-necked shakedown
room   possessions   person—then
entered the seemly company,
fellow indicted and co-conspirators.
Nuns, priests, friends
the inadmissible evidence of their lives
vivid as blowing flowers in a dustbin
(the big eye outside, the praying mantis).
Word went around quietly,
we have bread and wine!
That unwinking eye
glassing over with boredom
the mice in all seriousness played
the Jesus game.   A reading from Ezekiel
on the doomed city.   Silence. Philip whispering over the bread
(a con, a magian), over the "Mt. Dew" tin can.
We broke and passed the loaf, the furtive hands
of endangered animals.

My body given for you.

My blood outpoured.

Indictable action!

As in the first instance of vagrant Jesus,
in whose flesh rumors and truth
collided; usual penalty, rigorously applied.

My friends, it is the savor of life
you passed to me; vines, the diminished loaf
lost hillsides where the sun
sets the grapes beating like a hive

of human hearts; Cornell gorges, the distant sea
Block Island swung like a hammock from its moorings—
I come to myself
a beast in a shoe box
sport
of the king of the cats

No One Knows Whether Death, Which Some in Their Fear Call the Greatest Evil, May Not Be the Greatest Good

It may be expedient to lose everything.
The moon says it, waxing in silence, the fruit of the heavens,
     Grape vine, melon vine.
    Autumn upon us, the exemplar, the time of falling
One who has lost all is ready to be born into all:
    Buddha moon   Socratic moon Jesus moon
      Light and planet and fruit of all:
"Unless the grain falling to earth die, itself remains alone"

The Cross as Military Decoration

The bust of a beribboned military man
stands, close up, like a platonic daemon
while the brush stokes him out
of invisibility
the horizontal color bars
mark him like a chart
of the elements of creation—COMPLEAT AMURRICAN
He bears the cross: a Junker
military variation
its origin and occasion unknown to me.
The logical genius, however, the inversion
of original intent, strikes home hard.
You must give credit—the world is possessed
of both cunning and courage, all the way.
It is not sufficient—if myths are to abide
hot eyed, pristine—to tinker with good intent
less good, partial good, worldly good, etc.
No, the gods must be put to the wheel
The divine be enslaved. Thus the Book of Revelation.

The radical content and method of evil
the Unholy Spirit, the Abomination in the Holy Place
the powers and dominations, clue
to the perversion of right order.
Apart from such a vision, I challenge you
doctors of the mind's large spaces, lead me
into the heart of the century's deluge
and out again. Or create
simple trust in primary words and meanings
and consequent conduct in accord
with holy living and dying.
Jesus is murdered, the first victim
of the hands he freed for service.
The generals take up the cross, the croix de guerre.

Game time, the church's princes,
impresarios of evasion, line up
with battle doves: the gorgeous cock
floats, a lost soul between *yes & no.*

A Salvation of Sorts

Freak: one marked by physical deformity,
         appearing in circus side show.

"We are made a spectacle before angels and men" in wheeled
         cages, part of the bloody train of history, its ersatz triumphs;
         A passing show, under the smoldering hangman glances of
         the crowd,
A harelip, a 3rd boneless hand, a hump, a tail
ridiculous, an object of scorn, an animal, at distance from the
         Human, the usual, the manageable

         —parents, peers, whole men & women, culturally secure,
         religiously at peace, conjecturing silently on the origins,
         deviations, hebetude, fate, folly, folderol of
         the procession of freaks.

Misfits in the real world, fit only for death
         aberration, to those whose self-understanding is a silly putty,
whose holy spirit is the latest noisome social myth.

Jesus is the original misfit in the real world,
         fit only for death.
A misfit in that world which deceit, violence, fear, lust,
         pride of life have fitted unto themselves
         —in order a "fit" men and women for a life which is quite literally
          an ante-
         room of death, a rehearsal for hell
making the round square and the square round the short
         long and the long short
         so that all, all die
         in that auto-da-fe
         forbidding stature   nobility   uniqueness   cheerful &
         intriguing diversity.

A Reading (sort of) From Paul's First Loving Letter to Friends on the Greek Coast (& to us)

For those at the wheel of juggernaut, careening downhill out of
all control—for them the cross of Christ is of course so much
hokum.

But to people of soul, the cross is a sign of power.
So we read in the oracles, I will show how absurd is the
Wisdom of the wise, why all the prudence of the prudent comes
to a zero.

Indeed, where are they when the chips are down—all those
prestigious profs, those incumbents of endowed chairs, those who
sit high on their sacred haunches?
They run for the cellars when risk is in the air, they snigger in
their beards at the sight of young men standing firm, they
sneer at students and activists and those who refuse the death
game as a "way of life."
They snap their fingers and cluck with professional disdain, looking
up with dead eyes from dead tomes: *what gives with these
malcontents, these arrogant interlopers, these destroyers of our
value free turf?*

Their sacred books, the latest noisome absurdity from the cellar
labyrinth of the Doctor of Rodents . . .
Well, they can't understand, or more to the point, they refuse to
understand, power, wisdom, powerlessness, folly . . . Who will
help them unravel the truth?

Then—ourselves, outsiders, agitators, felons, freaks, makers of
music and poetry, given to giving, existing quite modestly in all
circumstances, refusing a helping hand to no one
in the special sense that everyone is special—called, we think, to
do a quite simple thing.

Plucked by the hair out of that mordant pride-ridden mass, our
bodies and spirits stroked like instruments by his hand
to make his music, to be his voice—
Listen
      Only
            Listen

Come, Dear Reader, Stand Breathless Before This Blinding Logic

(One day in prison, while having a dental exam in the dental clinic, Dan had a massive allergic reaction to a shot of novocaine and almost died.)

I may be forgiven the reflection: *medicine is politics.*
I had rather stretch out on my iron cot & phase out
before ever again
needles or neutralizers
of Doctor Niteshade.
The Confucian logic imminent to *"don't get sick in prison"*
must be enlarged to: *"don't get sick in America."*
Events introduce the dicta 1 to another like the
2 sweaty palms of priest and mortician, meeting with blind
vermicular logic
over the cemetery fence
where I or mayhap you, cher lecteur
for real
play dead

Skunk

The only fauna admitted
to the widespread country zoo
(every animal in his natural
habitat, no visible bars)
was an unloquacious
bumbling skunk.
He crept in under the full moon
like a moon thing, eyes
dazed, moonstruck. Limped
along unhandily, as though
on 5 feet or 3, footsore.
Looking for what?
We wished
he would breathe deep
as an ancestor, metamorphose
10 times his size
piss high as a Versailles fountain
his remarkable musk perfume.
We didn't want additional
prisoners, even dumb ones.
If they must come, atavistic,
mystical, then let them be
spectaculars, trouble-
shooters.

O skunk, raise
against lawnorder,
your grandiose
Geysering
stinking
NO!

A Desert Painting I Saw in Here, Badly Reproduced

(While in Danbury Prison in 1971, Dan received a friendly letter of support from the great artist, Georgia O'Keefe in New Mexico, who was also a friend of Thomas Merton.)

It is undoubtedly required
all one's life long
to plod about, useful
as a sourdough's mule, the prose
of one's flat feet, inmost
ruminations, matching
the splayed line
of an ass's back,
going
returning
(if lucky)
bowed like a shot bow,
under the hundredweights
of some el dorado.

Prose sometimes
yields to poetry
but only in the broken
jawbone of an ass
jawbone of a man

Friend, ghost
Georgia O'Keefe
put a desert
rose
in that bone dry urn
and walk on

Letter from Prison to the Vietnamese Prisoners

1.

Dear friends, your faces are a constriction of grief in the throat
your words weigh us like chains, your tears and blood
fall on our faces. Prison, Vietnam; Prison, U.S.
Prison is our fate, mothers bear in prison,
our tongues taste its gall, bars spring up
from dragons' teeth, a paling, impaling us.
A universal malevolent will, crouched like a demon
blows winter upon us, stiffens our limbs in death, the limbs of
women and children.
Here, they hawk death in the streets, death in the hamburger joint
death in the hardware, death in the cobbler's hammer
death in the jeweler's glass, the classy showrooms of death.
Death, shouts the newsboy; death, oranges and lemons,
death in a candy wrapper.
Death, the cinema blares it: Death!
And beyond it all, out of sight and mind
like an aquarium at midnight, a terminal hospital
like the eyes of a captive tiger
a colony of golden eyes
of bees in their cells, the miser's mine of jewels
throttling the moon underground–
you and I
our eyes like grapes under the nailed boots
our "Why?" dragged in the dust, a flayed animal's entail
our "How long?" long as the lifeline thrown from God to Job.

2.

If I were free! the phrase flies from our minds
        like a two-edged sword, an apocalypse cutting us free.
If we were free!
        I would be your angel of deliverance
all my friends! between you and me the evening star arises, the jewel of
Buddha
        that compassionate mind encompasses the heavens!
between those hands, their flower like
        texture and repose
nothing, nothing is lost!
        the tears of mothers sting like scorpions
the scorpion's sting falls like a tear.
        The universal order, fragile as eggshell, broken by the hammers
of mad bombers, heals
        heals under that starry breath!

Lord Buddha, Lord Christ
        whose hegemony, time and this world
is a compassionate unending search
        east and west, sunrise, sunset,
for the least and lowliest, the wounded, the violated—
        they live in us, the lords and servants of time
we live in them, lords and servants of time.

And we shall break our chains like chains of sand
        the conniving dissolute
puppets, their power
        slumps like a rotten sawdust
their marauding hearts
        burst in a suppuration!
our mothers' ears, the Buddha's tears and Christ's

        anoint us like a chrism
the sweet earth, punished by ruffians' fists
        heals like a rising loaf, a bread of heroes
and we shall sit and eat, the poor shall gather

under those bells and tears
from graves, ditches, huts, camps and caves
        from the ends of the earth, from air and sea
the wretched, the maimed, the blind, the halt
        the dead, lively, retiring, joyous as grasshoppers–Buddha and
            Christ,
Lord and servants of creation
        multiply that loaf in lotus fingers
the loaf of existence
        our immortal joy, flesh and family and tribe and nation
all things made new!

3.

In that day the ingathering, but first the scattering
        in that day the banquet, but first the starvation
In that day the freedom, but first the prison
        in that day the healing, but first the torture
In that day the music, but first the mourning
        in that day the justice, but first the false judgement
In that day the rebirth, but first the bloodletting.

4.

        We must remember, great Buddha said, the place, the person, the time, when we first sat at table together. And the first generation remembered.
        The second generation forgot the time. But they remembered the house, and their brothers' and sisters' faces. And great Buddha said, it is enough.
        The third generation forgot the hour and the house. But they

sat with their brothers and sisters, here or there, now or then. And great Buddha said,
it is enough.
        The fourth generation forgot the hour, the house, and the faces

of their brothers and sisters. And great Buddha wept.

In the fifth generation, everyone was a stranger. Men and women were violated and tortured and outlawed. And great Buddha perished. He died, a nameless peasant, in the general conflagration. He was buried in a common grave. And the earth was void.

5.

If the birth of a child
is sufficient reason
to trim the lamps
of the universe, to grace
seasons in a wedding garment,
to wreathe in smiles
our stiff jointed discontent–
then it must be insisted
with equally rigorous logic;
the murder of a child is sufficient reason
to burn like trash or offal
those hunting licenses
that go by the civilized
euphemism, "draft files," to endure
imprisonment, loss of repute
the stigma of Cain
branded by the perfumed hands
of judges, politicians and church men
on the forehead of Abel.

In a time of sanctioned
insanity, sane conduct
is an indictable crime.
In a time of omnicompetent

violence, compassion
is officially intolerable.
In a time that celebrates
the apotheosis of Mars,

Christ will languish
on ice for the duration.

Let us liberate reflection
that many branded verdant tree
from its plague of befouling apes–
abstraction, inflation,
mock heroism, mock victimhood.

We;
fed, clothed, housed
solicitously as the last
handful of survivors
of an endangered species.

It is hard in America, hard
even in American prison
to take death seriously.

Not hard for you, dear friends.
Official solicitude
evaporates with the distance.
For chairman Caesar or Christ,
the messianic legions
kill with an equal fervor.
In either case, you are honored
though ignorant of your honor;–
our superior motivation–
Pax Americana,
your bones to make our bread.

A.J. Muste said it: "We need a foreign
policy for the children." Exactly
Thus.

The death of one child
brings down the universe.
It is honorable to nurture

even in prison, that endangered
flame, to mingle if so required
one's unwavering purpose
like an eagle's, with that
bereft nest fallen life.

Foreign, domestic policies, idem.
I.e., the nearest child is the furthest.
The nearest of blood is not
thereby most dear.
American airmen dumping
their liquid fire upon faraway
hamlets, bear in breast pocket
Kodak prints of their children
Thus far corruption on high
of the call and course of the blood.

It is snowing tonight as I vigil.
The first white fall of winter
bitterly cold. I think on
of the fevers and horrors of Con Son.[1]

No to their No.
YES to all else.

1. [*Con Son was the Vietnamese prison island where the tiger cages were discovered.]

The Risen Tin Can

1.

Toward the near end of the prison graveyard
   stands a frantic caterwauling machine that flattens tin cans.
Its iron flail beats the air to death
   even when no forage intervenes.
Let us consider as poets do, the rightful synecdoche of the situation.

   We prisoners are so to speak, tin cans
emptied of surprise, color, seed, heartbeat, pity, pitch, frenzy
   molasses, nails, ecstasy, etc., etc.,
destined to be whiffed and tumbled into elements of flatland
   recycled, dead men's bones, dead souls—

now the opposite of all this is the shudder and drumming feet
   of the risen tin can
over the hill, into the sunrise
   the tin can contains, grows wings, he writes poetry!

This is the year of the RISEN TIN CAN, in the Vietnamese sense.
   REVOLUTION REFUSAL REBUTTAL POETRY.
When I was a tin can, I thought like a tin can, I looked like a tin can, I
spoke like a tin can.
   Now that I am a man, I have put away the things of a tin can
tin armaments, tin hearts, tin bells, rin-tin-tin gross national tin Ameri-
can tin.

No.
   It is expedient that the glory of God be not
melted smelted milled rolled.
   It is required that mere humans
even though with hanging head and drooping codpiece
   persuaded in contrariety to nature

of the intrinsic genetic inferiority
  solar surfaced
  and O so cheap definitive solution
of TIN—

It is expedient
  that mere men and women prevail
in face of the idol of Scissors Alley
  that hundred pincered crustacean can-and-man opener.

But I digress.
  the unforgiveable sin against the unholy Spirit
is the metamorphosis of tin
  into humanity
of which one instance: the writing of a poem.
  Shaking of foundations! It is not to be borne
that sounding and tinkling tin
  unzipped, emptied of its regal redoutable guts brains gore
should arise to the phoenix form of the twice born.
Celebrate it! An ivory stick on the Ethiopian drumhead
  the sweet tactile frenzy of B.B. King.
The puma's meeeooow of a steel band
  Catgut reborn!   Tin renascent!   Us resurrected!

E contra
  The Neanderthal triumph of the century beyond reasonable
Doubt is *Homo Danburiensis*

On the one hand
  the starched ars and starved brain of the cosseted correctionist
barking violations of the penny ante whipping out his tape
measure against the turds of the circus flea.
Then
  the raddled crook, unselfknowledgeable as an ass's elbow
rounding the dice, squaring the roulette, night and day stuffing
his kicked tail into his parched mouth. Prayer: *O keep me from
Chrissake awakening!*

It is recounted in the old legends that a child came unannounced among the uncopacetic beasts who thereupon discovered unlikely good things in one another, and wrath laid aside, fed, slept, foraged, wandered together, claw to fleece, tooth to feather.

The moral by gentle implication: the great Braggart and Beast himself, in comparison with whose ravenings the bestiality of beasts is a rare and mystic dance, might one day make peace as he perennially has made war.

Meantime the claims of the kingdom of death are beyond doubt total. They totalize and mobilize unman for their surrogate. Henceforth in tribute to the Great Pretender, one must walk on garbage, feed on ugliness, break stones by day and grind his molars by night.

His keepers march like articulated tin can sandwich men parading the First Command of the Lost Way: Be Like Me!

But

Let a blade of grass intervene, a vagrant lustful loving frenetic stammer arise in one; let him remember his lost friends, the cords of Adam, let a single bird cross his stared sight—

Let a single countervailing voice, color, feeling, sound—

All is undone

The sweet world is suddenly at hand, a NECESSARY ANGEL, BE UN-LIKE   CONNECT   I AM THE WAY   FREE EVERYONE   SHANTI SHANTI

Dear friends,

The Great Amortizer is at the door, syringe in hand.

He parts his face like a dead sea into: benevolence or murder
When he looks benevolent he means murder
When he looks murderous he means business
Business is good; you or someone else; viz—
He freezes your rent, he is burning someone's hut
He cures your cancer, he is filling his germ bottles
He worships on Sunday   Buddhists die for it.
This is called Caesar's karma.   It says: when you're a god,
You got responsibilities to your constituents.   Or
Some eggs may hatch but kitchens are for omelets or
If you can't take the heat don't lay an egg.
Thus the GREAT EQUALIZER decrees that some be tranquilized

And others freneticized, that there be generals and hoplites,
Winners and losers, Caesars (1 each) and slaves and keepers (of course)
and kept.
   Now it is a matter of imperial indifference whether you and I, cits,
dimwits, midges, near zeroes, non-heroes, whether we exist or no. But one
thing is clear: in our regard the myth of
Genesis has been turned around. Henceforth to read:
   In the beginning was Skinner's labyrinth.
The furry humanoids, deloused, decorticated, lobotomized, housed, fed,
schooled by the state
   Totally environmentalized   a synthesis of formally partial structures
(university, madhouse, prison, cinema, food trough, sex bed, church)
these scamperers and scavengers by dint of expertise and electrode have
learned

   when to fear when to love when to piss when to feed when to praise
when to—

What one might miss in their makeup (were he a backward looker, did he
dare search for certain nearly submerged characteristics of the tribe) is a
certain

Light in the eyes ('like shining from shook foil'), a plumbless interiority,
a tease and come on, something funky in youth, wrinkles as of laughter
about aged brows, a sip in your eye look of fire and ice.

OR at the least a glimpse of Edens lost a look of scarce contained grief, as
for other shores horizons estuaries, 'blue remembered bill,'

Yes—outraged love.

But no.
Bugged brainwashed buggered beggared besotted
Out of head and heart
Or let us say, so nearly
Out of head and heart
As to make no wit difference
To cast no grain of grit

In the armored almighty progress
Of the warmongering worm
NO. SO.
HIS ALTITUDINOUS ARSITUDE, SPITTLE THE FIRST,
ANNOUNCES FROM THE
IMPERIAL BUNKER: THE ALTERNATIVES ARE HEREBY
EXPUNGED.   KAPUT.

2.

Well almost.   Then again hardly,
Let us coolly, hardily
to fields away
make hay under the arc
that fans out, dawn
after hit and run dark.

3.

No to their NO.   YES to all else.

4.

It is Christmas
The pride of peacocks
The birth of a child
His many forms
rising swaying around him
like eyes in feathers
dances harvests brides
resurrections
and underside
His shadowed
befallings
Pray: those eyes
touching our eyes
Make us that human

December 2, 1971

One of them, a benign corrupt cop
with the face of a bishops' crook
locks me in, jocund at midnight.

Goose pimples, recognition
an Auschwitz moment
as if a renegade Jew
ushered his rabbi, with a flourish, a persuasive
push
into
"our best yes sir absolutely Grade A reserved oven."

Rehabilitative Report: We Can Still Laugh

In prison you put on your clothes
and take them off again.
You jam your food down
and shit it out again
You round the compound right
to left and right again.
The year grows irretrievably old
so does your hair burn white.
The mood: one volt above
one volt below survival,
roughly per specimen, space
sufficient for decent burial.

One Tries Hard to Mean These Words

Let us pray:
Forgive the big ones Father
who pull down   capricious wreckers
your mild and serviceable earth.
See deep   perplex long above
the plumbless pit of their wrongdoing
who devise   triumphant   cast in face
of you and yours   their tricky and tinny wares
dare fashion yes   to your thunderstruck gaze
idols   foul proximates
through clacking jaws to mime   mock you

Nevertheless
Forgive them Father straightway   hard and fast
bind up voracious wounds   for surgeon appoint
the meek of the earth   their hands
acquainted   as yours   with wounds   empty
of base-won gain.   Groans of the sinner
Groans of the healer   resound in you
concomitant   a second birth.
Bear us a new heart   Majesty   save
all things your tears and mirth called forth

It Was a Dry Year, Followed Unexpectedly by a Deluge

I couldn't for life or limb
shake a verse out of my
bag of tricks-
all wrong, all awry.

Then along came
Holy Mother State
humming an executioner's song;
she laid a claimant paw
on my sorry sack

And lo!, I can't
for the life of my soul
stop
singing it out.

In Jail We Had a Glimpse of the Sky

Majestic, undefiled
Clouds lord it overhead—
out of sight, out of mind

and who are we? and who are we?

In nature's lexicon
of reason and unreason—
in the mind's store
of wisdom and mad omission

what abides   what abides?
Great spirit, greater reason.

The root has touched rock.
We abide. We abide.

Zen Shovel

We dug a grave
On the White House Lawn
The fuzz were furious
dragged us away

But the little shovel
an industrious angel
went on digging
to judgment day

Down down it dug
and down and down
Up up it piled
that bloody spoils

And the angel whispered
to my puzzled soul
The further you dig
      into origins
the deeper deeper
      origins get.

One Thinks of Friends in Trouble Elsewhere, or; Change the Regime but Keep the Prisoners by All Means

The new political prisoners were given the task
of whitewashing the walls of the cells
polluted, pockmarked by the despair
of political prisoners of the old regime.
The same cells, it goes without saying.

The new political prisoners were given the choice
of whitewashing the slogans of the old regime
of preparing the ideology of the new regime
or residing indefinitely in the whitewashed cells
of political prisoners of the old regime—
the same cells, it goes without saying.

The lies were different, it goes without saying
until you examine them; then they were the same.
The prisoners were different, it goes without saying
until you examine them; infected wounds,
malnourishment, broken jaws, then they were the same.

The cells were different, whitewashed
odorless, it goes without saying—

until the new political prisoners scratched their coda
with bloody fingernails, and found
like a buried city or the cry of walled in prisoners—
found the lives, the torture, the outcome were the same
like the fingers that make a word
and the fingers that make a word
(yours, that blood brother named you)

in two sides of a crazy mirror.

I Hope and Pray This Doesn't Happen to Me

The poet recanted
They hacked off his fingers
and gave him a signet ring

The poet recanted.
They tore out his tongue
and crowned him their laureate

He was then required
to flay himself alive;
two houses of congress
applauded, they dressed him
in the Aztec cloak of immortals

The poet surrendered his soul
a bird of paradise
on a tray of silver held
in his two hands

His soul flew away;
The poet
by prior instruction
vanished where he stood.

On Being Asked to Debate H. Kissinger

When I sat down
they said with relief,
he's sat down at last.
But I hadn't. I was off like a shot put
and over their walls.

When I grew silent they said,
we've convinced him at last.
But they hadn't. I beckoned my soul aside
Come! Pick apples, feed on your vision.

Then I stopped breathing.
They said in relief,
we can breathe again in the world
and deceive with virtuous tongues
and kill with immaculate hands.

And they could, they could. Except
for these lines, those apples, that vision.

Wherein Are Explained My Reasons for Going From the University to the Pentagon, and Breaking the Law, Georgetown University Having Accepted Gross Millions From the Tyrant.

Because I don't want to look like the nose of the shah.

Because I don't want to look like the lapdog of the shah's sister.

Because I don't want to look like a serpent's tooth.

Because I don't want to look like a bureaucrat's belly stuffed with hunting licenses.

Because I don't want to look like the whites of the eyes of the dead, or a flag of truce.

Because I don't want to look like an odorless armpit, or a war on dirt, or a born again briefcase.

Because I don't want to look like an abortionist's pail, or a bishop's crook, or a crooked bishop.

Thank You, Your Point of View Is Certainly Interesting, If Somewhat Bizarre. Are there Any Questions?

The suburbs are sad as death
The university slumps on its arse
money dreaming of money.
Washington D.C., a whitewashed sepulchre
awaits the diggers of history
side by side, tombs, slums, imperial empathy.

Amid all this
the transfixed tourists
the international pimps

The wheelers and dealers
rolling along like chariot wheels of fate
the faces like faces on dollars—

amid all this
did one original mind
cry out a gospel verse

Panic in the streets!
Tumbling whirlwinds!
The unbearable halo
of resurrected Christ!

Hiroshima

Does the poem come to nothing?
        Not to believe it.
Nor to believe, it comes to nothing
        not to despise or cast away –
        contempt, time wasted.

This is an absolute; an emblem.

A summer come to nothing?
Summer, '45, Hiroshima
The bomb believes it; city, come to nothing!
beyond doubt, shadow of doubt-
the children gone to shadow.

General pores over a map.
He lights signal fire. The plane
up and off. Incinerates
map, grid, north-south vectors, inches per miles,
people of paper.

An absolute, an emblem;
no life comes to nothing.

Millions of lives
turn sunward the axis of a dark century,
keep the clocks right, balance the scales
steer the stars.

Angels they are, myriad
guardians of Jacob's ladder,
their image, the unborn,
—were these visible and desired—
wanting us, awaiting us, and
every so slightly
evading like light
our aching arms.

Swords into Plowshares

Everything enhances, everything
gives glory—everything!

Between bark and bite
Judge Salus's undermined soul
betrays him, mutters
very alleluias.

The iron cells—
row on row of rose trellised
mansions, bridal chambers!

Curses, vans, keys, guards—behold
the imperial lions of our vast acres!

And when hammers come down
and our years are tossed to four winds—

why, flowers blind the eye, the saints
pelt us with flowers!

For every hour
scant with discomfort
(the mastiff's baleful eye,
the bailiff's mastery)—

see, the Lord's hands heap
eon upon eon,
like fruit bowls at a feast.

Prisoners in Transit

They took the prisoners, willy-nilly
on death's own outing
shod like gray horses
jump suits pied like Mardi Gras
& curses & groans & ten pound shoes
& starts & stops
at every
station of the cross
across Wm Penn's
sylvania

'Here's where that first trouble –
shooter started his last mile,' the guard yelled
through his bull horn mouth—

'& here he did a phony fall—
gaining time was all

'& here is was
he rained like a red cloud
& here
we built his everloving ass
an everlasting memorial—

'this mile square Christian tomb
& closed the book

'You may all come down now
Take a 3 to 10 year
close look.'

My Brother's Battered Bible, Carried Into Prison Repeatedly

(Philip Berrigan spent over 11 years of his life in prison for civil disobedience to war and nuclear weapons, and every single day, studied his Bible. Dan began his homily at Phil's funeral with this poem.)

That book
livid with thumb prints,
        underscorings, lashes—
I see you carry it
into the cave of storms, past the storms
I see you underscore
like the score of music
all that travail
that furious unexplained joy.

A book! The guards
shake it out for contraband—
the apostles wail, the women
breathe deep as Cumaean sibyls,
Herod screams like a souped up record.

They toss it back, harmless.
Now, seated on a cell bunk
you play the pages slowly, slowly
a lifeline humming with the song
of the jeweled fish, all but taken.

For Philip in Prison

Not a day passes
I'm not caught up
in awe of it, the mastery—

as though, manacles sprung,
hands steady, sure,
in prayer and single mind
You, protagonist,
appointed the way.

I summon
Bonhoeffer, Jagerstatter-
who knew, who cared, when the blade fell
and the burned bones, boxed, sealed,
stamped FINIS, were cast in the Styx?

It's not fame, I know
you look toward, but soul.
So you shine, you tower like a stele
amid ruins unbroken, your soul
incised with scenes
from a broken life,
its Easter aftermath.

You
precious beyond words,
a gold bell in a wasteland
telling, tolling
the lost word *human*.

I stammer and celebrate, both,
the grief, the glory-
that signet set
in God's right hand,
dazzling
creating yes,
you anew.

Your Second Sight

(for Philip)

Walking by the sea
I put on
like glasses
on a squinting
shortsighted soul—

your second sight

and I see
washed ashore
the last hour of the world—

the murdered clock of Hiroshima.

The Verdict

(for Philip and the Pax Christi-Spirit of Life Plowshares, North Carolina, 1994)

The first day, my brother stood   .
      Sun shed dark
      And leonine stood beside.

The second, I followed, somewhat.
      The third to weeks' end
      I leave to you to know.

Leave it to him,
      His dignity, care, cure and—crime.
Something seen, said, done. Lips moving
      as though under water,
      words Himalayan,
      air thin, hardy
      birds faint and fall.

Let's sit here and wait—
all we may, for the end.
obey the prophets who say, wait
      the benchwarmers, beggars.

look, against all evidence, sun
shakes the dark once again.
      Stands
            to say so.

The Opposite

(for Philip and the Pax Christi-Spirit of Life Plowshares,
North Carolina, 1994)

Writing. I think: here's my hand
grown older, no matter. Weaving this web
like any spider, called words.
      Here, there, ranging, hello brother.
No matter who—my brother.

What's the opposite hard consonant
      to web, web, airy weaving?

What's the wholly opposite, what's
      all teeth, edgy, fricative,
      so frontal and free
      it breaks the metal cuffs of sheriffs,
      gives wrists their hands, hands their
      paintings, pianos, poems—

hand to hand, the children,
the dance of time
      yes, and
no need of no,
      after years of no

The Prisoner, the Cave

(for Philip and the Pax Christi-Spirit of Life Plowshares, North Carolina, 1994)

Ancients are writing with pencil stubs
scriptures in a cave.
What will be, what was
is, is, is in the cave.

Patience, a crystal, tells the time;
        that a cry, How long O Lord. That
        and no reply. None,
        and the outcry!

The parchment unrolls as they write—
        a sky, a beyond,
        a flying carpet, a throne
        whence issue thunders; Thus Sayeth.

Love one another, they write. They love.

        The cave is a pock on the moon.
        The moon wastes and wanders,
        a sea guarding its salt.

        Unrolled one day, the scroll
        will stutter, whisper, keen, thunder—
        too low a pitch for humans,
        lions plotting
        the last day of the lamb;
        a pitch too high, angels
        rehearsing apocalypse.

The Gift

(for Philip and the Pax Christi-Spirit of Life Plowshares,
North Carolina, 1994)

It's measureless
　　　only the image, Son
of the ineffable, takes its measure.

　　　like this:
　　　　　joined hands, hardly seen
　　　(dusk to dark on the instant)
　　　behind bars, beyond all barring
　　　a beseeching: have mercy
　　　　　　on the merciless!

　　　Like this, the measure:
　　　　he casts ahead like a fly fisherman—
　　　torment, truth. The take.

I Want You Free

(for Philip and the Pax Christi-Spirit of Life Plowshares, North Carolina, 1994)

Intemperate, temperate be damned.
    I want tempers riled, want
    vile matters resolved.
    I want you free.

    (No urge
to wax metaphysical, metaphorical
like puppeteers in pulpits—
    'Of course you're free')

      Justice?
The word's a smear or sneer,
    the locks guttural as guards.
      no key turns, no tongued
freedom bell intoning 'free!'
Nothing. Bars adamant
    as just held, withheld.

    Nothing?
    No.
    My love, the poem.

A Few Gifts for the Prisoner

Send him the sea, a bearded mime
mimicking lambs and lions

Send the sun
betokening variety and
crystalline steadfastness

Send one or two gestures of children
seizing tossing, meandering———
like the prisoners, making
much of little

Send an episode
of Luke's gospel of healing
let the prisoner hear that gift
on ward, hands incorrupt, empty.

And in and out of his cell
send a flea circus trooping
too small for the guard's gimlet.

Let Christmas come around
for the prisoner alone
cold, deprived, true.

And the angel
who succored Peter in chains—
the angel enters
the prisoner's soul, whispers
magisterially, not yet, no,
not yet.

Poverty

A prisoner is very poor
1 face, 2 arms, 2 hands, 1 nose, 1 mouth
Also 3 walls
1 ceiling
10 or 12 iron bars—
then if lucky
1 tree
making it, making it
in hell's dry seasons

I almost forgot—
No legs!
Contraband! Seized!
They stand stock still
in the warden's closet.
There like buried eyes
they await the world.

Penalties

You in prison
I, so to speak, at large
I taste the penalty too.
Half a world, half a loaf
like a two-legged dog I saw once
body precariously balanced
Left-
        Front-
                Leg
Right-
        Hind-
                Leg
tottering about
image of half a soul, so to speak
alive in the so-called world
the hunger, the half a loaf
called life.

What Marvels the Lord Works for Them (Psalm 126)

When the Spirit struck us free
we could scarcely believe it
for very joy. Were we free
      Were we wrapt
in a dream of freedom?
Our mouths filled with laughter
our tongues with pure joy.

The oppressors were awestruck; what marvels
the Lord works for them!
Like a torrent in flood
      our people streamed out.
Locks, bars, gulags, ghettoes, cages, cuffs
a nightmare scattered

We trod the long furrow
slaves, sowing in tears.
A lightning bolt loosed us.
We tread the long furrow
      half drunk with joy
      staggering, the golden
      sheaves in our arms.

Hymn to a New Humanity

(El Salvador, Nicaragua, and the U.S., Summer, 1984)

The guns are common as stacked firewood,
      and as cheap.
They are common as walking sticks carried by the aged and infirm.
There is a gun for every contra who carries a gun.
There are toy guns for infants and flowery guns for little girls.
To the delight of children, there are clown guns that go
      !popopop!—and wouldn't harm an insect.
There are chocolate guns for Easter; guns that spout
      water and guns that sprout a parasol for rainy days.
The guns, of course, have eyes. The guns of the Guardia
      Civil have ears. And there are merchant guns that
      smell a dollar, like a miser's nose in a sirocoo of money.
And statemen's guns, equipped with silencers, sheathed
      like their owners in raw silk, a spiffy outfit.

There is a rare gun, a gun of dark rumor. The ultimate
gun, the gun named god. Like god, it has never been seen,
      virtue of the invisibility, it must be believed in.
Somewhere, no one knows where, whether on land or sea
      or in the air, this gun is sequestered, stroked, nourished by the
      hands of servitors.
Like the queen bee of hell, it waxes in the dark, fed on morsels of children,
      boiled eyes and pickled ears. It is indifferently a carnivore, a flori-
      vore, a faunivore.
This is a metaphysical gun. It renders all other guns,
      together with their makers and users, redundant.
It is aimed at the heart of history, the secret wellsprings of life.

Innocent as the three famous monkeys, guns
      see no evil, speak no evil.
Guns believe in guns, guns hope in guns, guns adore guns.
      In the new dispensation, these are honored as

theological virtues.
There are loving marital guns. They vow fidelity, each to
        The other, at the altar of revolution. Thereupon they
        are blessed by clerical guns in white surplices.
Also guns are laid on the table at Mass, next to the bread
        and wine; then they are said to be consecrated guns.
There are guns held by sheep and guns held by goats. To
        the former Christ says: Come ye blessed. To the
        others: Depart from me. Or so it is said.
In El Salvador, the guardia peer out from behind the
        smoke windows of vans, like Mississippi sheriffs
        behind their shades; the look of a leveled gun.
In Nicaragua, the guns have learned to smile; like
        cornucopias of metal, they whisper promises:
        Dear children, trust us; from our barrels pour the ABC's,
        medicines, a blessed life. Trust us, stroke us,
        vote for us. In our dark void is concealed all
        your future.

It has proved embarrassing on occasion that the Christian
        documents are recusant on this matter of guns.
        Exegetes, artists, poets, intellectuals have been moved
        in consequence, to create as it were, a contrary hypothesis.
        The empty-handed Christ,
        they declare, "would have," "must have," "might have"
        carried a gun. Or at the least, he favored their legitimate use—
        just guns for just causes.
In the older iconography, the hands of Christ are by no means empty.
        They bear the bounteous fruit of a storied imagination:
        shepherd's staff, teacher's scroll, a lamb or two, wheat, chalice.
        Now these sublime and simple things are lifted from his hands.
        Even that bloody heart; livid as a skinned plum, to
        which his index pointed as a very *sigillum* of love—
        it is torn from his side.

We have in fact imagined a better way of imagining him
        than he was capable of.
What has occurred is roughly this. There came a time
        when it was no longer possible to venerate the older
        symbols of the holy and the human. Our species
        evolved, in accord with exigencies of time and place.
A new human emerged from the tired womb of tradition;
        a tradition which here and there, through service of
        lip and heart, had preached a cult of—gunlessness.
A gauche ideology indeed! On its behalf, believers failed
        to coin a usable term. Nonviolence? It was a clumsy
        transliteration. They were gunless, that is all.
Our own times signaled a breakthrough. Guns were no
        longer mere instruments of bleak choice. They were
        now simply a matter of wholeness, morphology. To this point,
        to be gunless corresponded, in the ethical sphere, to a mishap of
          nature;
        an armless or legless or sightless being; one lacking
        in a substantial component of the human.
Thus, to bring a long matter around, a fresh light is cast
        on a very old subject.
Meantime, it must be admitted that a few recalcitrant priests and their sequences
        spurned the light. In public places they intemperately cried out
        the old credo to their gunless god. They were dealt with,
        summarily.
Our genetic leap postulated a new icon. The older images
        had died with their god. They were best buried, once for all.
In this matter, we were relentless: new humans, a new god.
Our theology produced a generation, not of iconoclasts,
        but of inspired entrepreneurs. We now possess, in
        plazas and shadowy corners, in discourse and dance,
        the Christ we have come so richly to deserve.

Pie in the Sky

*(In the summer of 1992, the Governor of Arkansas and Presidential
Candidate, Bill Clinton flew home to witness the execution of
lobotomized Ricky Rector. Led from his cell to the electric chair, the
prisoner left the pie from his last meal in his cell, intending to eat it after
his execution.)*

Someday somehow I'll get me
makeup of that pie
Rick shoved forkfuls of
into his soon to be
resurrected tummy
treadin, yumyumin among the
dead men walking
& hummin no doubt, and strumming
"America the Beautiful."

Why just imagine, the same
current that baked the All-
American confection
sent Rick shooting praises
altitudinous, the pie
like unto him combusted
      like unto him alas
      eternally
unconsumed.
Who I ask my soul
the savvy baker of this
(turned executioner—
but don't
dwell on this or that—
apples, lard, flour,
rolled out flat—
blood, bone, pore addled brain,
recipe close kept

As a sheriff's keys—
        who lo, hath wrought this wonder?

Why poor Rick doesn't know
his ars from a baked apple.
Then drag him outta there for
fifty quickened paces,
a made-up word sufficing
urging 'C'mon Rick, quick like—
ex-e-cu-tion, ex-ha-la-tion,
ex-cavation'—
then KABOOM!
what he don't know won't hurt him.

Sure kid cross my heart we'll
bring you right back here yer
just desserts awaiting.

Miracles

Were I God almighty, I would ordain
rain fall lightly where old men trod,
no death in childbirth, neither infant nor mother,
ditches firm fenced against the errant blind,
aircraft come to ground like any feather.

No mischance, malice, knives.
Tears dried. Would resolve all
flaw and blockage of mind
that makes us mad, sets lives awry.

So I pray, under
the sign of the world's murder, the ruined son;
Why are you silent?
Feverish as lions
hear us in the world,
caged, devoid of hope.

Still, some redress and healing.
The hand of an old woman
turns gospel page;
it flares up gentle, the sudden tears of Christ.

Etty Hillesum

(died in Auschwitz, Nov. 30, 1943)

"Here goes then," wrote this woman I never heard of.
And "I don't want to be safe, I want to be there."
Wrote this woman.

She is like a God I never heard of.
She is like a bride I never married.
She is like a child I never conceived.
Like death? Death she heard of

Death she walked toward, a child lost
in the glowering camps.
After years and years—recognition!

I heard a cry: "My child!"

The ineffaceable likeness. Death
her child, her semblable.
Wrote: "In such a world I must kneel. Kneel down.
But before no human." In the furnace
lust and its cleansing, birth and its outcome.
To kneel where the fire burns me, bears me.
Eros, God, Auschwitz.

      She wrote: "To live fully
outwardly, inwardly, my desire. But to renounce
reality for reality's sake, inner for outer life—
quite a mistake."

Wrote to her love: "Dear spoiled man
now I shall put on my splendid dressing gown
and read the bible with you."

O singer of songs of song,
O magnificat Mary,
O woman at the well of life!

You Finish It: I Can't

The world is somewhere visibly round,
perfectly lighted, firm, free in space,

but why we die like kings or
sick animals, why tears stand
in living faces, why one forgets

the color of the eyes of the dead—

Prayer for the Morning Headlines

MERCIFULLY GRANT PEACE IN OUR DAYS. THROUGH YOUR HELP MAY WE BE FREED FROM PRESENT DISTRESS . . . HAVE MERCY ON WOMEN AND CHILDREN HOMELESS IN FOUL WEATHER, RANTING LIKE BEES AMONG GUTTED BARNS AND STILES. HAVE MERCY ON THOSE (LIKE US) CLINGING ONE TO ANOTHER UNDER FIRE, TERROR ON TERROR, GRAPES THE GRAPE SHOT STRIKES. HAVE MERCY ON THE DEAD, BEFOULED, TRODDEN LIKE SNOW IN HEDGES AND THICKETS. HAVE MERCY, DEAD MAN, WHOSE GRANDIOSE GENTLE HOPE DIED ON THE WING, WHOSE BODY STOOD LIKE A TREE BETWEEN STRIKE AND FALL, STOOD LIKE A CRIPPLE ON HIS WOODEN CRUTCH. WE CRY: HALT! WE CRY: PASSWORD! DISHONORED HEART, REMEMBER AND REMIND, THE OPEN SESAME. FROM THERE TO HERE, FROM INNOCENCE TO US: HIROSHIMA DRESDEN GUERNICA SELMA SHARPEVILLE COVENTRY DACHAU HANOI KABUL BAGHDAD. INTO OUR HISTORY, PASS! SEED HOPE. FLOWER PEACE.

Harm Not the Trees

Down, they come down. What's an elm, or ten
or for that matter, a bow legged old woman

afoot painfully along Roach Run, what's she worth?

Down, a hundred year tree.
Sawdust stands in a column, dissolves

in choked air. A sun shot day, the elm root
splayed our level, a huge starfish, a silver star

like the one inset in marble
in Bethlehem grotto. *Hic Jesus Natus Est*

who died on a tree. This wooden star
sprung from convulvuses

cruciform on the warm earth, wet
with a hundred rings of life—

the tears of Jesus, a pathetic fallacy
a summoning device for times too tragic, awry.

Dip hands in the essence. It flows
three or four weeks of spring, the time

when in south land, mocking birds toss
sleepless with ecstasy.

O may all creatures live!

Ambition

I wanted to be useless
as life itself; so
I told the president so
and told the pope so
and told the police so

& one & all chorused
like furies, like my friends
And who told you so?

The dead told me so
the near dead; the prisoners
all who press faces
against a wall of glass
a grave, a womb's thrall.

I read their lips, alas.
I told the poem. So.

Less Than

The trouble was not excellence.
I carried that secret,
a laugh up my sleeve
all the public years
all the lonely years
(one and the same)
years that battered like a wind tunnel
years like a yawn at an auction
(all the same)

Courage was not the fault
years they carried me shoulder high
years they ate me like a sandwich
(one and the same)

The fault was—dearth of courage
the bread only so-so
the beer near beer

I kept the secret under my shirt
like a fox's lively tooth, called
self-knowledge.

That way
the fox eats me
before I rot.

That way I keep measure—
neither Pascal's emanation
naked, appalled
'under the infinite starry spaces'
nor a stumblebum

havocking
in Alice's doll house.

Never the less!
Summon
Courage, excellence!

The two, I reflect, could
snatch us from ruin.

A fairly modest urging—
Don't kill, whatever pretext.
Leave the world unbefouled.
Don't hoard.
Stand somewhere.

And up to this hour
(Don't tell a soul)
Here I am.

Apartment 11-L

These are the rooms I go from.
An angel commands me: Go from here.
I go
to break the bones of death, to crack
the code of havocking dreams. I go from here
to judgment, to judges
by Roualt, Daumier, Goya,
their hammer crack of doom.
I go. Then I'm told
by a guardian angel of the room I'm told—
when you go from here
faces of those you love
turn to the wall and weep.
I have an angel's word.

And when I return
older, sad at times, so little of death undone,
despite all sacrifice and rage
when I return,
Lo, something savory, exotic,
steams in a pot, the table fitly laid.

And the typewriter's iron mask
melts in a smile and the keys
like a lover's hands
compose a love letter:
Welcome.
   Believe.
     Endure.

Equilibrium

(for John Dear)

Equilibrium—
favored word of mystics;
Equilibrium
in all save love.

We, land creatures
essaying
adverse elements—

Our high wire act,
brief, dangerous—
one foot firm
one in midair.

A few are skilled
breathtakingly.
              They run
that equator, as though riding
a burning arrow.

             (In all things
tried, true, above all
in love.)

Regard not only
the arrow, but the gradual
spent force of the string
let go.
             How graceful
the bow at rest;

                    But
O under pressure, like
the bold breath
of Creator Spirit –
                    Twang!
                    and torn
from thin air,
a song of songs!

September 27, 1971

A Chinese ideogram
shows someone
standing
by his word.
Fidelity. Freedom
consequent
on the accepted
necessity of
walking where
one's word
leads.
Wherever.
Hebrew prophets and
singers also
struck the theme;
bodies belong
where words
lead
through the com-
mon run of exper-
ience be
that stature
shrinks as
the word
inflates.
The synthesis;
No matter what (or
Better) *never*
the less

There's a Deed Floating Somewhere

For every 10,000 words
there's a deed
floating somewhere
head down, unborn

Words can't make it happen
They only wave it away
unwanted.
Yet Child, necessary one
unless you come home to my hands
why hands at all?
Your season your cries
are their skill
their reason.

Somewhere In the Middle

My life goes like this
The Christians decided to make a Jew of me.
I ended up around someone's neck
an albatross or crucifix
anyway, a 'saving metaphor,' never a glimpse of the author's
sour sweet face, though his heart
hammered away—
Providence, you're providential!

And the Jews?
When I came around, they laid it down hard;
Love us, love yeretz Israel!
When I stammered out
certain distinctions between the blood stained faces and the blood stained earth
they'd have none of it, fists came down.

So
my destiny (big deal) is
marginal as a cockroach or a crucifix.

I wander the strait and narrow
Broadway, among the stupefied and stoned
the mutterers and mugged
hanging on like the tails of kites
to mad time and its drovers, up wind and down
Broadway, the ravenous kites, trucks, trailers—

I'll add this: if you sought me
You'd find me
cross hatch in the narrow strip
between cross draughts of hell
cross legged on a filthy bench
forever, next to nothing.

Like a lotus there, or a sunrise—
You've never seen on the Big Apple
such a smile.

Taking Stock

Taking stock of
such as myself—

and enduring as I must
the dark quandary
named Here, named Now—

until a knell sound and the sea gives up its dead
and continents
heave like a pummeled dough
with exiles revenant—
and eternity's throat
like a bell take note
'all all is well'—

look, it were better
in bitter meantime
to smile
and lift a glass—

the starts and stops,
brisk, becalmed,
distempered, sweet,
the sojourn short or long—

the outcome
in better hands
than ours.

Block Island Cottage

(A few years after Dan was arrested at the home of theologian William Stringfellow on Block Island, RI, Stringfellow built a little cottage for Dan on a cliff overlooking the ocean, which Dan then visited every few months for the rest of his life. On the white wall in the main room, he painted by hand in black ink this poem.)

Where this house dares stand
at Land's End
and the sea turns in sleep
ponderous   menacing
and our spirit fails and runs
—landward seaward askelter—
We pray You
Protect
From the Law's Clawed Outreach
From the Second Death
From Envy's Tooth
From Doom's Great Knell
All
Who Dwell Here

Each Day Writes

In my heart's core
ineradicably, what it is to be human.

Hours and hours, no sun rises, night sits
kenneled in me: or spring, spring's
flowering seizes me in an hour.

I tread my heart amazed: what land,
what skies are these, whose shifting weather
now shrink my harvest to a stack of bones;
now weigh my life with glory?

    Christ, to whose eyes flew,
whose human heart know, or furious or low,
the dark wing beat of time: your presence give
light to my eyeless mind, reason to my heart's rhyme.

If

If I am not built up
bone upon bone
of the long reach and stride of love—

If not of that
as stars are of their night;
as speech, of birth and death; thought
a subtle paternity, of mind's eye—

If not, nothing.
A ghost costs nothing.
Casts nothing, either; no net,
no fish or failure, no tears like bells

summoning across seas
the long reach and stride of love
dawning, drowning those black waters.

Insight

When I look, I see
I've spent my life seeing—
under that flat stone, what?
Why that star off kilter?

Turn Turn! I intoned, and
out of the stone there stood
What-Not in a white garment.

Jacob's ladder descended
(the angels holding steady)—
I mounted and I
saw
What

Chicago, Holy Week

A thought:
We were done with winter
But the great lake leapt to the sky and down
a warrior at our throat.
We were stuck
like tires in muck.
Back to back
cold shouldered December jostling April ungodly
a grimace.

A thought:
We were done with death
the long long run of it
the planet tilting crazy
winds wicked utterly
the long run of the drama drains the heart
wreckage of Genesis
death row upon row
the Calvary route
the trio bad, cursing good,
and the center pole
run through
the one we long to be done with
desperate
no second chances
death in the offing
if we could
if only He would
like the one to right or left of His hand
die
and be done with

Chariot

We're sane as the dawn
that consents, creates
time and again, our world.

Let's help, let's flog.
The flanks of the chargers
that lift the sun aloft
against all odds—
horses, horseman Apollo
so beautiful
so overrated.

I'd rather be at mercy
of someone less appalling
less breakneck.
Someone—steadfast
even stuck.

I'd say we're stuck.
I'd say—that's a start.

Maybe—go from there?
Maybe
Someone's at our side who
(get up, up!)
died under the wheels.

The gods of the 1980s

The god of expectations made money like mad, made
        money like butter in a churn, poured it out
like butter over popcorn, on the deserving and the
        covetous alike. And was blessed and applauded,
and that was a good year.

The god of approximations made the kingdom almost come.
There were merely brush wars, small wars,
minor contusions on the world map. But
        by and large, the sanctuaries were full and
the priests preached on and the collections came in
and the officials gave good example from the front pews.
And that was a good year.

The god of contemplations made humans spin
like spinning rainbows. Seated on a bed of gold
        Like a lotus on a pond, he intoned:
"You think therefore you are." So they thought
and thought and they were and they were.
And that was a good year.

The god of executions staggered down the road,
dragging a plank of wood heavy as a plowshare.
like a plowshare the plank made a furrow;
from the furrow sprang useless lives,
        talking skulls, disconsolate dragons,
        teeth on edge. A girl named Cassandra
        brought up the rear, raving into the wind.

All this is of no moment and went
almost unnoticed. Except for this:
with regard to money, war, thought—

that was a very bad year.

The Economy Is Bullish

I hear how Mammon prospers
        from the woman on the street
            who has nothing but the street

Each night she rolls up the pavement
        like a goose-down blanket.
            All weathers, she's cozy there.

   Each day
in the brows of power brokers,
   she wheels and deals
      humming along
with the whirring Stock Exchange.

   She wears triage like a billboard,
     tricked out in ticker tape
     laying bets like Mother Courage—
a hundred to one, a square meal, she moans
   c'mon baby, give!

   Then
   off she pushes in harness.
she's tomorrow
   pushing today away.

   She's the next war.

My Brother Prisoner in Transit

(March 17, 2001)

What logic cannot do, and mourning might
or might not (chancy, you're stuck on a trestle,
a train galloping behind, that's the world)

—a poem will.

      Give it time, give
the mind entire.

      I did. An hour, two. A lamp lit,
and my brother's face stood,
an emblem of courage unvanquished,
of faithful faith.

Brother, where you are I would be, your gift and mine
acknowledged or not (but who of us greatly cares?)

      Four brute walls hem me in,
bars forbid the season,
unblinking cyclops sting the eye blind.
      And loneliness, a ghastly
guardian mastiff, baying; You're mine, mine!

Christ confers it, this harsh salvation, this plucking
by hair of head away, far from the crooked age.

Cruelties bless, disguised.
      Lockup, you look up
in prayer, the open sesame of mystics, hermits.

We live
a drama of end-time, of time and scoundrel world
surpassed.

What comes of it, this submission?

Time cannot tell, eternity is mum.

But
sure to be, a promissory note
steeped, signed in Christ's blood.

Willy nilly,
an unlikely evangel, the Judge intoned it aloud.

After

(September, 2001)

When the towers fell
a conundrum

Shall these from eternity
inherit the earth,
all debts amortised?

Gravity was ungracious,
a lateral blow
abetted, made an end.

They fell like Lucifer,
star of morning, our star
attraction, our access.

Nonetheless, a conundrum:
did God approve, did they prosper us?

The towers fell, money
amortised in pockets
emptied, once for all.

Why did they fall, what law
violated? Did Mammon
mortise the money
that raised them high, Mammon
anchoring the towers in cloud,
highbrow neighbors
of gated heaven and God?

"Fallen, fallen is Babylon the great . . .
They see the smoke
arise as she burns . . . ."

We made pilgrimage there.
Confusion of tongues.

Some cried vengeance.
Others paced slow, pondering

—this or that of humans
drawn forth, dismembered—

a last day – Babylon
remembered.

The Catholic Bishops Approve Bush's War

(November, 2001)

Lest I merge
with mountains that surely will fall,
their decrepitude my own –

Lest I walk shod
in blood of Abel crying from the earth,
'My tantamount, my brother, my undoer' —

Lest for eons I must carry
Rachel's sacrifice, her tears my albatross –

Lest I the Christ
disavow,
And Him who shackled there
I drag through sludge
of cowardice and dismay—

Lest weighed, I be found
wanting –
no guest of heaven,
a ghost, and no egress
from foolish trumpery of time –

Lest I disappear, down down
the 110th escalation
of pride,

and truncated, eyeless, soulless,
be found
unfit for armed might
for rubble and America—

Lest I be sifted
like wheat or chaff,

and under a pall
(the appalling flag)

am borne away
piecemeal
to broken doorways
of sheol or limbo,

(the divergencies
not large, nor mine to choose) –

Lest I

Payment

(On Dr. King's birthday, 2000, Fr. Daniel Berrigan, Fr. John Dear, Fr. Simon Harak, and other friends were arrested for protesting at the USS Intrepid War Museum in Manhattan. They didn't know that all the jails in Manhattan were full that day. They were handcuffed, chained together, put in a van, driven around town in search of a vacant cell for the rest of the day. Finally, around 3:00 a.m. in the morning, they were forced to march several blocks in the freezing cold weather, chains connecting them at the ankle and waist, to the Tombs where they stood in a crowded cell for the rest of the day.)

It was something akin
to paying your way

(no saving metaphor
to be sure)

Paying
for the next mile
the next heartbeat
the next sunset

something owed life,
the sheer beauty,
yes, the heartbreak—

small price, all said
handcuffed,
driven in a chain gang
across Manhattan
at cold midnight,

something paid
to strike
the manacles Christ bore
and bears in the world.

Does the metaphor befit?
I'm unsure.

That way it might.

Days on an Island in January Will Do This to You

Sun, moon, storm
nothing last
nothing should, they say in the city
whose clocks run fast, run past
like people.
Yesterday snow owned the yard like a pall on a dead face
slowly drawn
Imagine you saw the snow ever so slowly draw breath an inch or two
above the face
you were so close to who just went
you hardly breath.
The walls, stone walls
big stones, each a guard
facing, if so a face, facing away.
Today, thawing snow creeps close, curved, cold as a serpent's lip
for survival
A thin white line, then a dark line,
Impressionists caught it,
careless and caring
the shadow of stone owns like God
all that barely makes it this far.
and out at sea,
waves a league long arrive from Portugal
and die like near-heroes ashore.
Spectacular!
They resemble the pharaoh's chariots, horses, and men tumbling down
scriptures, expendables, watery warriors
another, then another
tries, and dies.
Obsessed, you say?
Give them credit!

That willfulness marching straight up the cliff
to return you, every one of you
back, the pharaoh barker,
back where you belong.

Good Friday

You come toward me
prestigious in your wounds
those frail and speechless bones.

Your credentials:
dying somberly for others.
What a burden—
gratitude, fake and true vows,
crucifixes
grislier than the event—

and then the glory gap—
larger than life
begetting less than life,
pieties that strike healthy eyes
blind: believe! believe! Christians
tapping down the street
in harness to their seeing eye god.

Only in solitude
in a passing tic of insight
gone as soon as granted—
I see you come toward me
free, free at last.

Can one befriend his God?
The question is inadmissible, I know.
Nonetheless a fiery recognition
lights us;
broken by light
making our comeback.

Facing It

Who could declare your death,
obedient as Stylites, empty as death's head,
majestic as the world's sun   moving
into night?

It was a hollow death; we
dread it like a plague. Thieves die this way,
charlatans, rejects. A good man's thought recoils;

to grow old yes,
home and faces
drifting out of mind. Abrupt violence yes
a quick mercy on disease
but not, not this; the mother's face
knotted, mottled with horror,

time's cruel harrowing
furies at the reins of fortune
wild horses dragging
the heroic dishonored body on time's ground.

O for an act of God! We cry, before death utterly
reduce to dust
            that countenance, that grace and beauty.

But
come wild hope, to dead end. War, murder,
anguish, fratricide.

No recourse. The case of Jesus Christ
is closed. Make what you will

desire, regret, he lies
stigmatized, a broken God
the world had sport of.

Risen?
We have not turned that page.

Resurrection

To raise the huge question
heave it like a boulder
far from the cave mouth closed
like a dossier of the convicted
guilt and best dead
the question to which there stands alas in death's arrogant dominion
only a hint
a meager dawn illumination
I circle the tomb wearily

The Magdalene saw a gardener
John, Peter ran head to head
Crucifixion sets friends fleeing
Resurrection and we crowd the rent tomb
fear and awe contending.

I wish, wishing
would bring you into being
my being
You who are
like the lorn father of a demon-ridden child

I believe,
Help thou
my unbelief
Or Graham Greene, "This saves me,
I don't believe my disbelief."

Through walls
You slip in or away
like an airstream through air.
And that smile so seldom before
lingers lingers
essence of rainbow unspent

You cast no shadow.
What can this mean?
Would you walk that road twice?
In new existence, do you summon tears?
Once you were clothed in imperfect flesh.
Is the perfect bearable?
Do you imagine other ways of being God?
Contemplative bones
easeful as lotus
a cresols half-slipping out of time
a Buddha under a banyan tree?

The Face of Christ

The tragic beauty of the face of Christ
shines in our faces.

The abandoned old live on
in shabby rooms, far from comfort.
Outside, din and purpose, the world, a fiery animal
reined in by youth. Within
a pallid tiring heart
shuffles about its dwelling.

Nothing, so little, comes of life's promise.
Of broken, despised minds
what does one make—
a roadside show, a graveyard of the heart?

Christ, fowler of street and hedgerow
cripples, the distempered old
—eyes blind as woodknots,
tongues tight as immigrants'—all
taken in His gospel net,
the hue and cry of existence.

Heaven, of such imperfection,
wary, ravaged, wild?

Yes. Compel them in.

Word

I'm seeking a word
unknown
and I unable

Imagine, 84, seeking a word!
Like an infant, the first word of the tongue
from milk, murk and memory

How do I make a word
which must, at all cost, be the first?

A word beyond foretelling
like eyes unborn
whose color unknown
unable
will paint the colors of the world

Knowledge

Everything known beforehand

Except
the hand from a cloud
releasing rain's largesse,
blinding rain like sheaves.

Except
the hand from the ark
freeing a dove in air

Except
the dove
blind, affrighted, tossed
on a watery void

Except
You
lodged there, secret,
the world's nest egg

from whose birth
rises our only
Hand Ark Dove

Zen Poem

How I long for supernatural powers!
said the novice mournfully to the holy one.
I see a dead child
and I long to say, Arise!
I see a sick man
I long to say, Be healed!
I see a bent old woman
I long to say, walk straight!
Alas, I feel like a stick in paradise.
Master, can you confer on me
Supernatural powers?

The old man shook his head fretfully.
How long have I been with you
and you know nothing?
How long have you known me
and learned nothing:

Listen; I have walked the earth for 80 years
I have never raised a dead child
I have never healed a sick man
I have never straightened an old woman's spine

Children die
men grow sick
the aged fall
under a stigma of frost

And what is that to you or me
but a turn of the wheel
but the way of the world
but the gateway to paradise?

Supernatural powers!
Then you would play God
would spin the thread of life
and measure the thread
5 years, 50 years, 80 years
And cut the thread?

Supernatural powers!
I have wandered the earth for 80 years
I confess to you,
sprout without root
root without flower

I know nothing of supernatural powers
I have yet to perfect my natural powers!

to see and not be seduced
to hear and not be deafened
to taste not be eaten
to touch and not be bought

But you—
would you walk on water
would you master the air
would you swallow fire?

Go talk with the dolphins
they will teach you glibly
how to grow gills

Go listen to eagles
they will hatch you, nest you
eaglet and airman

Go join the circus
those tricksters will train you
in deception for dimes—

Bird man, bag man, poor fish
spouting fire, moon crawling
at sea forever—
supernatural powers!

Do you seek miracles?
listen—go
draw water, hew wood
break stones—
how miraculous!

Listen: blessed in the one
who walks the earth 5 years, 50 years, 80 years,
and deceives no one
and curses no one
and kills no one

On such a one
the angels whisper in wonder;
behold the irresistible power
of natural powers—
of height, of joy, of soul, of non belittling!

You dry stick—
in the crude soil of this world
spring, root, leaf, flower!

Trace
around and around
and around—
an inch, a mile, the world's green extent—
a liberated zone
of paradise